Japanese
cocktails

Japanese
cocktails

Over 40 highballs, spritzes
and other refreshing
low-alcohol drinks

Leigh Clarke

RYLAND PETERS & SMALL
LONDON • NEW YORK

Senior Designer
Sonya Nathoo
Commissioning Editor
Alice Sambrook
Production Manager
Gordana Simakovic
Editorial Director
Julia Charles
Art Director
Leslie Harrington
Publisher
Cindy Richards

Photographer
Alex Luck
Drink Stylist
Tara Garnell
Prop Stylist
Luis Peral
Indexer
Vanessa Bird

First published in 2019 by
Ryland Peters & Small
20–21 Jockey's Fields
London WC1R 4BW
and
341 E 116th Street
New York, 10029
www.rylandpeters.com

10 9 8 7 6 5 4 3 2 1

Text copyright © Leigh Clarke 2019
Design and photographs copyright
© Ryland Peters & Small 2019

The author's moral rights have
been asserted. All rights reserved.
No part of this publication may
be reproduced, stored in a retrieval
system or transmitted in any
form or by any means, electronic,
mechanical, photocopying
or otherwise, without the prior
permission of the publisher.

ISBN: 978-1-78879-074-1

A CIP record for this book is
available from the British Library.
US Library of Congress CIP data
has been applied for.

Printed in China

IMPORTANT RECIPE NOTES
- For best results, serve all mizuwari and highball ingredients chilled.
- All ice should be freshly made and crystal clear.
- Each cocktail recipe serves 1.
- Where very small measurements occur, they have been provided in grams as there is no suitable Imperial conversion. Digital scales that can measure in small increments are essential.
- Edible flowers used to garnish must be food-safe and pesticide free.
- Raw egg whites should not be fed to the elderly or anyone with a compromised immune system.

Contents

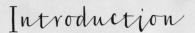

Introduction

In Japanese culture, bartending is regarded as an art form and much pride is taken in perfecting the craft. Drinks are mixed with precision, and the focus is on clean, well-balanced flavours, rather than a high alcohol content.

This book takes inspiration from the Japanese style of bartending to bring you a range of cocktail recipes featuring fresh fruity flavours as well as more savoury tastes like matcha, sansho, miso and sesame. Japanese liquors such as sake and plum wine provide ample opportunity for exciting new drinks to try, as well as twists on well-known classics.

The iconic mizuwari (meaning mixed with water), is a popular way of drinking in Japan and it has also inspired many of the recipes in these pages. This style of long drink is becoming increasingly in demand in cocktail bars around the world, as it offers a tempting alternative to high strength and often unbalanced drinks for those who would prefer to pace themselves. Some short drinks are included here too, but these are again well-balanced and served in small measures.

Cordials

Freshly made fruit cordials are used throughout the book to add depth of flavour and sweetness. These cordials will keep for up to 3 weeks refrigerated, meaning they can be used multiple times in different recipes. Sugar is added to the cordials by weight, because the amount of sugar in different fruits varies. Simply weigh the strained liquid from the fruits, then add the specified percentage of sugar by weight for each recipe. For example, if the recipe states to add 1% sugar and your juice weighs 100 g, you would need to add 1 gram of sugar. Digital kitchen scales that can measure in small increments are an essential piece of equipment here. Acid is then added to most of the cordials, which makes for a cleaner flavour and keeps them fresher for longer. If you don't have time to make a cordial from scratch, you can use a good quality store-bought variety instead, but you may need to adjust the other ingredients slightly to balance the flavours.

Sugar syrups

Simple sugar cocktail syrup is widely available to buy or you can easily and more cheaply make it yourself. Simply place some filtered or bottled water in a saucepan and add the appropriate amount of caster/granulated sugar (whether the same amount as the water for a 1:1 syrup or a third of the amount of the water for a 2:1 syrup). Set over a low heat and stir until the sugar has dissolved. Let the syrup cool before bottling, it will keep for up to 2 weeks refrigerated.

Acidulated sugar syrup

This syrup is used as a brightener in some drinks, as you would use a squeeze of lime in a highball. Simply stir in 6.4 g citric acid and 3.2 g malic acid to 150 g/5   oz. sugar syrup (with a 2:1 sugar to water ratio) off the heat until dissolved. Let the syrup cool before bottling, it will keep for up to 3 weeks refrigerated.

Acidulated honey syrup

The honey brings a richer, more caramel-like flavour to this syrup. Stir in 125 g/4   oz. runny honey to 250 g/9 oz. sugar syrup (with a 2:1 sugar to water ratio) over a low heat until dissolved. Then add 3.1 g citric acid and 6.25 g malic acid off the heat and stir in until dissolved. Let the syrup cool before bottling, it will keep for up to 3 weeks refrigerated.

Mizuwari & Highballs

Nikka Coffey Mizuwari

Mizuwari cocktails originated in Japan as a way to celebrate and explore the complex flavours in whisky through controlled dilution. Made correctly, these highballs can showcase flavour notes otherwise hidden in the whisky. It is important that all the ingredients used in mizuwaris are well-chilled to begin with. Nikka Coffey, the whisky used in this recipe, is robust in flavour and almost bourbon-like in style, with hints of vanilla and toasted coconut on the nose, which work beautifully with the coconut water in this serve.

50 ml/$1\frac{2}{3}$ fl oz. Nikka Coffey Whisky

coconut water, to top up

thick lemon zest strip, to garnish

Fill a thin highball glass to the top with ice. Gently pour in the whisky and slowly stir $13\frac{1}{2}$ times. If the ice level drops, add more ice to fill the glass. Top up gently with coconut water, giving a final few stirs to combine the ingredients. Garnish with lemon zest.

Yamazaki Mizuwari

Big tropical fruit notes feature in this drink, along with an almost silky mouthfeel. The soda also heightens the aromas of toasted nuts and dried fruits in the whisky.

50 ml/1²⁄₃ fl oz. Yamazaki 12 Year Old Whisky

soda water, to top up

dehydrated pineapple slice, to garnish

Fill a thin highball glass to the top with ice. Gently pour in the whisky and slowly stir 13¹⁄₂ times. If the ice level drops, add more ice to fill the glass. Top up gently with soda water, pouring down a bar spoon to protect the bubbles. Lightly stir to combine the ingredients and garnish with a dehydrated pineapple slice.

Mizunara Mizuwari

Look for the notes of green apple in this whisky, which really come to the fore with the addition of the soda water.

50 ml/1²⁄₃ fl oz. Chivas Regal Mizunara Whisky

soda water, to top up

edible flower, to garnish

Fill a thin highball glass to the top with ice. Gently pour in the whisky and slowly stir 13¹⁄₂ times. If the ice level drops, add more ice to fill the glass. Top up gently with soda water, pouring down a bar spoon to protect the bubbles. Lightly stir to combine the ingredients and garnish with an edible flower.

All Malt Mizuwari

A big, biscuity whisky, the All Malt makes for a toasty and rich long drink with great depth of flavour.

50 ml/1²⁄₃ fl oz. Nikka All Malt Whisky

soda water, to top up

wheat/barley ear, to garnish

Fill a thin highball glass to the top with ice. Gently pour in the whisky and slowly stir 13½ times. If the ice level drops, add more ice to fill the glass. Top up gently with soda water, pouring down a bar spoon to protect the bubbles. Lightly stir to combine the ingredients and garnish with a wheat/barley ear.

Chita Mizuwari

With notes of fresh citrus and honey, Chita is a beautifully light and bright whisky and makes a perfect highball serve.

50 ml/1²⁄₃ fl oz. Suntory Chita Whisky

soda water, to top up

fresh mint sprig, to garnish

Fill a thin highball glass to the top with ice. Gently pour in the whisky and slowly stir 13½ times. If the ice level drops, add more ice to fill the glass. Top up gently with soda water, pouring down a bar spoon to protect the bubbles. Lightly stir to combine the ingredients and garnish with a fresh mint sprig.

Black Grape Whisky & Dry

The dry tannins from the grape skins give refreshing bite
to this fruity highball serve.

30 ml/1 fl oz. Black Grape Whisky*
15 ml/½ fl oz. Black Grape Cordial**
10 ml/2 teaspoons Dolin Blanc Vermouth
soda water, to top up
thinly sliced black grape, to garnish

Pour all the drink ingredients, apart from the soda, into a highball
glass. Add some cubed ice and stir, then top up with soda water. Stir
gently again to combine and garnish with thinly sliced black grape.

Black Grape Whisky: 20 g/¾ oz. sliced black grapes,
400 ml/1⅔ cups whisky Add the ingredients to a ziplock freezer
bag and remove all the air. Cook in a water bath at 52°C (125°F) for
30 minutes. Allow to cool, then strain through a coffee filter. Bottle
the whisky and keep refrigerated for up to 1 month.

**Black Grape Cordial:* 250 g/9 oz. seedless black grapes,
50% caster/granulated sugar by weight, 1% citric acid by weight
Extract the juice of the grapes in a juicer and strain until it runs clear.
Weigh the juice, then measure out 50% of that weight in sugar and
1% in citric acid and stir in until dissolved. Bottle the cordial
and keep refrigerated for up to 3 weeks.

Whisky & Fuji Apple

If you have never had a Japanese Fuji apple before, then it is worth making the following drinks just to try this amazing fruit! The skin can range from white to the deepest of pinks, and it has a unique floral taste.

35 ml/1¼ fl oz. Japanese whisky

75 ml/2½ fl oz. freshly pressed Fuij apple juice
(extracted with a juicer from 1–2 apples)

Fuji apple slices, to garnish

Add the whisky to a highball glass full of ice. Pour the pressed juice through a sieve/strainer into the glass. Garnish with Fuji apple slices.

Non-alcoholic Apple Spritz

20 ml/⅔ fl oz. Fuji Apple Cordial*
75 ml/2½ fl oz. freshly pressed Fuji apple juice
(extracted with a juicer from 1–2 apples)

50 ml/1⅔ fl oz. soda water

edible flower, to garnish

Add the apple cordial to a highball glass full of ice. Sieve/strain the juice into the glass. Top up with soda water and garnish with an edible flower.

Fuji Apple Cordial: 4 Fuji apples, 40% caster/granulated sugar by weight, 1% malic acid by weight Extract the juice of the apples in a juicer and strain through a coffee filter. Weigh the juice, then measure out 40% of that weight in sugar and 1% in malic acid and stir in until dissolved. Bottle and store the cordial in the refrigerator for up to 1 month.

Fizz & Fruit

Nashi Sour

A nashi is a beautifully crisp and juicy Japanese pear, with thirst-quenching sweetness and creamy-white flesh. Pear liqueur is used in this twist on a whisky sour to add crispness to the drink, which is then lengthened with soda.

40 ml/1⅓ fl oz. Chivas Regal Mizunara Whisky

10 ml/2 teaspoons Liqueur De Poire (pear liqueur)

30 ml/1 fl oz. sugar syrup (1:1 sugar to water ratio)

10 ml/2 teaspoons egg white

15 ml/½ fl oz. fresh lime juice

1 dash Angostura bitters

soda water, to top up

orange zest (squeezed and discarded), to serve

edible flower, to garnish

Combine the whisky, pear liqueur, sugar syrup, egg white, lime juice and bitters together in a cocktail shaker and dry shake without ice first to emulsify the egg white. Add some ice and shake again, then strain through a fine-mesh sieve/strainer into a glass tumbler and top up with soda water. Squeeze the orange zest to express the citrus oils over the drink and discard. Garnish with an edible flower.

Peach Bellini

There is an amazing sparkling sake called Shochikubai Shirakabegura Mio, which is available online and in Japanese food stores. Absolutely beautiful to drink by itself, it has a uniquely sweet aroma and bright fruity flavour, which also lends itself perfectly to a Japanese-style Bellini. For a cherry variation, use the Fermented Cherry Cordial (page 56) with 3 drops of rose water, in place of the peach cordial and almond extract.

25 ml/¾ fl oz. Peach Cordial*

2 drops almond extract

Shochikubai Shirakabegura Mio (or other sparkling sake), to top up

Add the cordial and almond extract (or rose water) to a stemless flute/tulip glass. Slowly top up with the sparkling sake and gently stir to combine.

*Peach Cordial: **12 ripe peaches, 50% caster/granulated sugar by weight, 1% citric acid by weight** Remove the stones from the peaches (but do not peel them) and pass through a juicer. Cover and leave the juice at room temperature for 24–36 hours until the flavour begins to turn slightly fizzy. Strain the juice and then weigh it. Measure out 50% of that weight in sugar and 1% in citric acid and stir in until dissolved. Bottle and store the cordial in the refrigerator for up to 3 weeks.

Yuzu Collins

The aromatic Japanese yuzu tastes like a combination of all the different citrus fruits rolled into one, and delivers a hugely refreshing zesty bite that pairs perfectly with gin. Good quality and reasonably priced yuzu juice was once difficult to source outside of Japan, but it is becoming more widely available – it can be found on souschef.co.uk and in Japanese grocery stores. Turning the juice into a cordial makes it last longer.

10 ml/2 teaspoons Yuzu Cordial*
10 ml/2 teaspoons store-bought yuzu juice
40 ml/1⅓ fl oz. gin
soda water, to top up

Shake the yuzu cordial, juice and gin together in a cocktail shaker, then strain over cubed ice into a collins glass. Top up with soda water and serve.

*Yuzu Cordial: 300 ml/1¼ cups store-bought yuzu juice, 150 g/¾ cup caster/granulated sugar Stir the sugar into the juice until dissolved. Bottle and store the cordial in the refrigerator for up to 2 months.

Melon Shandy

A shandy is a great way of having a beer with a little less booze, but they can often be too sweet. Here, a watermelon cordial is topped up with crisp Japanese lager. The homemade cordial harnesses the delicate fruit flavours and complements the lager without overpowering it. Yuzu cordial also works very well in a shandy, giving it a pleasant zingy edge.

25 ml/¾ fl oz. Melon Cordial* (or Yuzu Cordial, page 23)
25 ml/¾ fl oz. soda water
75 ml/2½ fl oz. crisp Japanese lager (such as Asahi),
to top up

Pour the melon cordial (or cordial of your choice) into a highball glass. Add the soda and stir gently to combine. Top up with the beer. Note: The key to a successful shandy is ensuring all elements are very cold before combining, so be sure to keep the soda, cordial and beer refrigerated. For a really refreshing serve, pop your serving glasses in the freezer first to make sure they're ice-cold, too.

*Melon Cordial: 500 g/18 oz. melon, skin kept on (galia melon or watermelon are both good options), 50% caster/granulated sugar by weight, 2% citric acid by weight Remove the seeds from the melon flesh and pass through a juicer. Strain the juice and then weigh it, then measure out 50% of that weight in sugar and 2% in citric acid and stir in until dissolved. Bottle and store the cordial in the refrigerator for up to 3 weeks.

Plum Wine Sour

This cocktail uses the acidity in both plum wine and rice wine vinegar instead of citrus juice to provide the sour element. You can buy plum wine from most large supermarkets or grocery stores – the Kikkoman brand is used here, which is readily available. The result is a delicious, slightly savoury sour. Spritz the drink with orange zest juices to boost the plummy flavours!

10 ml/2 teaspoons rice wine vinegar

20 ml/$^2/_3$ fl oz. plum wine

7.5 ml/1½ teaspoons sugar syrup (1:1 sugar to water ratio)

25 ml/$^3/_4$ fl oz. Japanese whisky

20 ml/$^2/_3$ fl oz. egg white

orange zest (squeezed and discarded), to serve

edible flower, to garnish

Combine the rice wine vinegar, plum wine, sugar syrup and whisky in a cocktail shaker. Add the egg white and dry shake without ice first to emulsify the egg white. Add some ice and shake again, then strain into a rocks glass over fresh ice. Squeeze the orange zest to express the citrus oils over the drink and discard. Garnish with an edible flower.

Stirred & Infused

Mandarin Gimlet

The first gimlet was created using lime cordial, but it is a style of drink that lends itself beautifully to any citrus fruit. Mandarin is used here to create a fragrant and zesty alternative. Mandarin leaves (used in the cordial) are found attached to the fruit when it is purchased from an organic market or greengrocer.

40 ml/1⅓ fl oz. gin (Nikka Coffey, if possible)
20 ml/⅔ fl oz. Mandarin Cordial*
mandarin zest, to garnish

Stir the ingredients with ice in a mixing glass, then strain into a chilled coupe glass. Garnish with mandarin zest.

***Mandarin Cordial:* 300 ml/1¼ cups water, 70 g/2½ oz. mandarin zest, 4 g mandarin leaf, 50% caster/granulated sugar by weight, 1% citric acid by weight** Add the water, mandarin zest and leaf to a ziplock freezer bag and remove all the air. Place in a water bath and cook at 52°C (125°F) for 30 minutes. Allow to cool, then strain the liquid through a coffee filter. Weigh the liquid, then measure out 50% of that weight in sugar and 1% in citric acid and stir in until dissolved. Bottle and store the cordial in the refrigerator for up to 3 weeks.

もちろん、それは<ruby>アヴァンギャルド芸術<rt>アヴァンギャルド</rt></ruby>だ、あの時代に一般の客もいた大衆もツワトよほどしっかりと文化の展開を追うことにあり、彼らにその意図もなかったのはまったくもって伝統の束縛を断ち切ろうとする強い確信が、彼にのである。ツワルトのデザインにおいてテクノロジーがとの主要な要因になっていないことは、

<ruby>若者<rt>もの</rt></ruby>たちが実験を行っていた当時、書籍タイポグラフィやレースの印刷技術で制約されていたというっってしかれ、彼らの実験的デザインでは、完成イメージを<ruby>手切り<rt>て</rt></ruby>貼りの手法で「構成」された後、金属凸版（イラストレーション複製技法）あるいは手間のかかる石版印刷の技法で<ruby>版下<rt>はんした</rt></ruby>また、オフセット印刷の発展のおかげで図像の複合から構成されるイメージの複製行程は大いに簡略化されたとはいえ、相変わらずモンタージュという時間のかかるやり方がこのようなイメージを制作する唯一の基本手段である。

ピート・ツワルトが『PTT（オランダ郵便電信電話会社）のための本』──1930年代後半から始まった郵便業務のための小冊子──で行ったとても有名なデザインでは、図や絵と

Shiso Martini

Shiso is a beautiful green and purple leaf used throughout Japanese cuisine. Its delicate flavour combines well with vermouth in this martini. The measure is kept small so that the drink doesn't warm too much in the glass.

50 ml/1⅔ fl oz. Shiso Vodka*
10 ml/2 teaspoons dry vermouth
small shiso leaf, to garnish

Place a small coupe glass in the freezer. Pour the vodka and vermouth into a mixing glass full of ice. Stir well, then strain into the frosted coupe glass. Garnish with a small shiso leaf.

Shiso Vodka: 300 ml/1¼ cups vodka, 3 g fresh shiso leaves Add the shiso leaves to the vodka and then leave to steep for 2 hours at room temperature. Bottle and keep in the refrigerator for up to 1 month.

Shiso Vodka Soda

Shiso is part of the mint family and has a unique grassy, peppery flavour. It gives a perfect little twist on this classically 'clean' drink.

40 ml/1⅓ fl oz. Shiso Vodka*
5 ml/1 teaspoon Acidulated Sugar Syrup (page 7)
soda water, to top up
edible flower, to garnish

Combine the shiso vodka and acidulated syrup over ice in a highball glass. Briefly stir, then top up with soda. Garnish with an edible flower.

Rice Milk Punch

The rice milk in this drink can be bought from any good Asian superstore. The astringency in the black tea mixed with the whisky splits the milk, and the milk solids are then removed, leaving just a hint of cream on the palate. As an optional extra to give another dimension of flavour to this drink, you can add 2 teaspoons sweet white miso to the bottle of rice milk and let it infuse in the fridge overnight. Clearspring do a great sweet white miso paste and it's available in most organic stores or online.

50 ml/1⅔ fl oz. Rice Milk-washed Whisky*
10 ml/2 teaspoons sugar syrup (1:1 sugar to water ratio)

Stir the rice milk-washed whisky with the sugar syrup over cubed ice, then strain into a rocks glass over ice.

***Rice Milk-washed Whisky:* 3.6 g/1¾ teaspoons loose black tea, 300 ml/1¼ cups Japanese whisky, 75 ml/2½ fl oz. rice milk** Stir together the tea and the whisky in a jug/pitcher and leave at room temperature to infuse for one hour. Stir the rice milk into the whisky and refrigerate until curdled and 'split' (this can take anywhere from 30 minutes to 3 hours). Strain through a coffee filter. Note: The milk-washed whisky may not be completely clear after the first strain, so pass it through the same filter again and it will get there! Bottle and store the whisky in the refrigerator for up to 3 weeks.

Matcha Milk Punch

Here, inspiration is taken from the Japanese matcha latte, which has become commonplace in the UK as a coffee alternative. Matcha has a gorgeous bright green colour, and a vegetal, almost savoury aroma with a sweet after-taste. Sweet, sharp raspberry essence complements the grassy notes of the matcha beautifully.

3 teaspoons matcha tea

300 ml/1¼ cups milk

90 ml/3 fl oz. fresh lemon juice

120 ml/4 fl oz. vodka

50% caster/granulated sugar by weight

1% citric acid by weight

2 drops raspberry essence per 600 g/21 oz.

green jelly, to garnish (optional)

In a large jug/pitcher, whisk the matcha tea into the milk until dissolved. Mix the lemon juice and vodka together, then stir into the matcha milk. Refrigerate until curdled and 'split' (this can take anywhere from 30 minutes to 3 hours). Strain through a coffee filter until completely clear (you may need to do this twice). Weigh the strained liquid and measure out 50% of that in sugar and 1% in citric acid and stir in until dissolved. Finally, add the 2 drops of raspberry essence per 600 g/21 oz. Bottle and store the vodka in the refrigerator for up to 3 weeks.

To serve, pour 150 ml/5 fl oz. into a rocks glass over ice and garnish with green jelly on a cocktail stick/toothpick, if you like.

Sesame Old-fashioned

Fat-washing is an excellent way to infuse flavours rapidly and effectively into a spirit. The concept is simple, take a flavour you would like to transfer, ideally in an oil or fat form and combine it with your spirit. Freeze overnight and then strain to separate the deposits from the alcohol. The rich, nutty flavour of sesame seeds is the perfect complement to whisky.

40 ml/1⅓ fl oz. Sesame-washed Whisky*
20 ml/⅔ fl oz. Nikka Coffey Whisky
10 ml/2 teaspoons sugar syrup (1:1 sugar to water ratio)
black sesame seeds, to garnish

Stir the ingredients over ice in a mixing glass for a minute, then strain over ice into a rocks glass. Garnish with black sesame seeds.

***Sesame-washed Whisky: 5 g white sesame seeds,
20 g/1½ tablespoons unsalted butter, 200 ml/generous ¾ cup
Nikka Coffey Whisky** Lightly toast the sesame seeds in a heavy-based frying pan/skillet over a low-medium heat. Add the butter and allow to melt. Pour in the whisky and stir to combine all the ingredients. Transfer to a freezer safe container, allow to cool and then seal. Freeze for 12–24 hours to allow the flavours to infuse. Pass the liquid through a coffee filter 1–3 times until the fat deposits are removed. Bottle the whisky and keep refrigerated for up to 3 weeks.

Miso Old-fashioned

Here are two riffs on the classic old-fashioned, a sweet white miso gives a subtle richness to the whisky, while peanut butter gives a deeper one.

40 ml/1⅓ fl oz. Miso-washed Whisky*

20 ml/⅔ fl oz. whisky

shiso leaf, to garnish

Stir the ingredients over ice in a mixing glass for a minute, then strain over ice into a rocks glass. Garnish with a shiso leaf.

Miso-washed Whisky: 1 tablespoon sweet white miso paste, 1 tablespoon butter, 200 ml/generous ¾ cup Japanese whisky
Heat the miso and butter gently in a saucepan until liquid, then stir in the whisky. Transfer to a freezer safe container, allow to cool and then seal. Freeze for 12–24 hours, then pass the liquid through a coffee filter 1–3 times. Bottle the whisky and keep refrigerated for up to 3 weeks.

Peanut Old-fashioned

40 ml/1⅓ fl oz. Peanut Butter-washed Whisky*
20 ml/⅔ fl oz. Japanese whisky

Stir the ingredients over ice in a mixing glass for a minute, then strain over ice into a rocks glass.

Peanut Butter-washed Whisky: 2 tablespoons smooth peanut butter, 200 ml/generous ¾ cup Japanese whisky Heat the peanut butter gently in a saucepan until liquid, then stir in the whisky. Transfer to a freezer safe container, allow to cool and then seal. Freeze for 12–24 hours, then pass the liquid through a coffee filter 1–3 times. Bottle the whisky and keep refrigerated for up to 3 weeks.

Iced Teas & Frozen Cocktails

Tokyo Iced Tea

A Tokyo iced tea is a twist on a Long Island iced tea which normally calls for luminous midori (melon liqueur) in place of tequila and is topped with lemonade. You might class it as a guilty pleasure for a night on the town. In homage to that drink, here is a version of a Tokyo iced tea, with light wine-based spirit soju as the base and a tart melon cordial. With soda instead of lemonade, it is more fresh and less sweet than the original.

40 ml/1⅓ fl oz. soju

75 ml/2½ fl oz. cold green tea

25 ml/¾ fl oz. Melon Cordial (page 24)

soda water, to top up

melon balls on a cocktail stick/toothpick, to garnish

Shake the soju, green tea and melon cordial in a cocktail shaker with ice, then strain into a sling or highball glass over ice. Top up with soda water and garnish with melon balls on a cocktail stick/toothpick.

Mandarin Iced Green Tea

Mandarin and honey go very well together, and this iced tea is wonderfully refreshing, great for making large batches of and serving to friends on a hot summer's day. For a non-alcoholic version, simply top up a measure of cordial with cold green tea over ice.

35 ml/1¼ fl oz. Green Tea Whisky*
15 ml/½ fl oz. Honey & Mandarin Cordial**
soda water, to top up
mandarin zest, to garnish

Pour the green tea whisky and honey and mandarin cordial into a highball glass over cubed ice. Stir, then top up with soda water. Squeeze the mandarin zest to express the citrus oils over the drink and use to garnish the glass.

*Green Tea Whisky: 500 ml/2 cups plus 2 tablespoons Japanese whisky, 5 g/2½ teaspoons loose green tea Add the ingredients to a ziplock freezer bag and remove all the air. Cook in a water bath at 52°C (125°F) for 30 minutes. Allow to cool, then strain through a coffee filter. Store the whisky in a sealed bottle at room temperature.

**Honey & Mandarin Cordial: 65 ml/2 fl oz. Acidulated Honey Syrup (page 7), 3 drops mandarin essence (available online) Simply mix together the honey syrup and mandarin essence. Bottle and store the cordial in the refrigerator for up to 3 weeks.

Peach Iced Tea

The peach is honoured in Japanese culture. It has its own holiday, and
is always the most popular flavour in Japanese soft drinks and confectionery.
Peaches and almonds are a classic flavour pairing, as the almond helps
to bring the deeper flavour notes of the peach to the fore. Sake adds bite
to this delicious cocktail and the green tea provides length and
refreshment. For a non-alcoholic version, simply top up a measure
of cordial with cold green tea over ice.

20 ml/$\frac{2}{3}$ fl oz. Peach Cordial (page 20)

3 dashes almond extract

35 ml/1$\frac{1}{4}$ fl oz. sake

cold green tea, to top up

fresh peach wedge, to garnish

Pour the peach cordial, almond extract and sake into a highball
glass over cubed ice. Stir, then top up with green tea. Garnish with
a fresh peach wedge.

Plum Iced Tea

Plum wine, also known as umeshu, is a delicious liqueur with a sweet fruity flavour. Here it balances the fragrant bitterness of black tea to make a refreshing and unusual iced tea. For a non-alcoholic version simply top up a measure of fermented plum cordial with cold black tea.

15 ml/½ fl oz. Fermented Plum Cordial*
15 ml/½ fl oz. plum wine
50 ml/1⅔ fl oz. cold black tea
soda water, to top up
fresh plum slices, to garnish

Pour the plum cordial, plum wine and cold black tea into a highball glass full of ice and stir. Top up with soda water and garnish with slices of fresh plum.

Fermented Plum Cordial: 100 g/3½ oz. chopped plums (stones removed), 5 g/⅕ oz. yeast (preferably White Labs sake yeast), 500 ml/2 cups plus 2 tablespoons water, 60% caster/granulated sugar by weight, 1% citric acid by weight Combine the chopped plums and yeast in a large mason/kilner jar, then cover with the water and stir. Seal the jar and leave to ferment at room temperature for 8–10 days. Taste every 2–3 days after the first 6 days – once the water tastes of the fruit and the flavour is intense enough, strain through a coffee filter. Weigh the fermented plum juice, then measure out 60% of that weight in sugar and 1% in citric acid and stir in until dissolved. Bottle and store the cordial in the refrigerator for up to 3 weeks.

Salted Melon Sake

Salt is a wonderful flavour enhancer and used sparingly it can really help to elevate sweetness in drinks. Here, it acts as a boost for the saline undertones in the honeydew melon and adds an extra dimension to this frozen drink.

¼ honeydew melon, peeled and chopped, seeds removed

70 ml/2⅓ fl oz. sake

15 ml/½ fl oz. lime juice

pinch of smoked or regular salt

20 ml/⅔ fl oz. Melon Cordial (page 24)

melon fan, to garnish

Add all the drink ingredients to a blender with 6 cubes of ice. Blend until smooth and pour into a wine glass. Garnish with a melon fan.

Frozen Yuzu Margarita

A well-made frozen margarita is easily one of the world's most loved drinks. London ramen heroes, Bone Daddies, have mastered the frozen yuzu margarita and this is a homage to that moreish margarita. Make a big batch and serve it at a ramen party.

20 ml/⅔ fl oz. store-bought yuzu juice

10 ml/2 teaspoons lime juice

15 ml/½ fl oz. agave syrup

50 ml/1⅔ fl oz. tequila

Add all the drink ingredients to a blender with 1 scoop of cubed ice. Blend until smooth and pour into a rocks glass.

Sparkling Sake Sgroppino

A popular summer drink in Italy, this version of a Sgroppino swaps the usual lemon sorbet for a tangy melon ice, which works in harmony with the delicate sparkling sake.

2 scoops Melon Sorbet*
15 ml/½ fl oz. vodka or gin (as preferred)
sparkling sake, to top up
lime zest, to garnish

Remove the sorbet from the freezer 10 minutes before you want to serve. Place two scoops of melon sorbet into a mug or glass and pour your chosen spirit over. Gently pour the sparkling sake down the side of the vessel to stop it over-foaming, until you reach about 2 cm/³⁄₄ inch from the top. Garnish with a strip of lime zest.

*Melon Sorbet: 1 honeydew melon, peeled, seeds removed and chopped, 100 g/½ cup caster/granulated sugar, 100 ml/⅓ cup lime juice Place all the ingredients in a blender and blend until smooth. Transfer to a freezer proof container and freeze. Stir the sorbet mixture every 3 hours, using a fork to break up any ice crystals, until smooth and frozen.

Black Sesame Sake au Soyer

This drink is a version of a classic cocktail that can be found in *The Savoy Cocktail Book* by Harry Craddock. The original calls for Cognac and Champagne, but this version uses Japanese whisky, sparkling sake and black sesame ice cream to create a delectable dessert substitute...

1 scoop black sesame ice cream (available from Asian grocery stores)

15 ml/½ fl oz. Japanese whisky

sparkling sake, to top up

Remove the ice cream from the freezer 15 minutes before you want to serve. Scoop the ice cream into a coupe glass. Pour over the whisky, then gently pour over the sake until you reach the edge of the glass.

Umami Adventures

Nori Martini

While most familiar as the casing for sushi rolls, toasted nori seaweed
has a complex salty flavour that works wonderfully well in a martini,
in the same way that a briny olive does.

30 ml/1 fl oz. nori-infused gin

20 ml/²⁄₃ fl oz. gin

20 ml/²⁄₃ fl oz. dry vermouth

dried nori strip, to garnish

Place a martini glass in the freezer. Stir the nori-infused gin, regular
gin and dry vermouth in a mixing glass over ice, then strain into your
frosted martini glass. Garnish with a strip of dried nori on the glass.

Cherry & Sesame Highball

Sweet, juicy cherries are here combined with nutty sesame to give a rounded, multi-layered flavour profile. The skin to flesh ratio of cherries is pretty low, so it can be difficult to extract a strong flavour from fresh cherries. Frozen cherries, on the other hand, are perfect for a cordial as they have a large amount of locked in flavour and sugar.

20 ml/⅔ fl oz. Fermented Cherry Cordial*

40 ml/1⅓ fl oz. Sesame-washed Whisky (page 36)

soda water, to top up

edible flower, to garnish

Pour the cherry cordial and sesame-washed whisky into a highball glass. Stir to combine the ingredients, then top up with soda water. Garnish with an edible flower.

Fermented Cherry Cordial: 250 g/9 oz. frozen cherries in liquid, 5 g/⅕ oz. yeast (preferably White Labs sake yeast), 100 ml/3⅓ fl oz. water, 1.5% caster/granulated sugar by weight, 1% citric acid by weight, 0.5% malic acid by weight, 0.5% almond extract per 200 ml/6¾ fl oz. juice Combine the frozen cherries and yeast in a large mason/kilner jar, then cover with the water and stir. Seal the jar and leave to ferment at room temperature for 8–10 days. Taste every 2–3 days after the first 6 days – once the water tastes of the fruit and the flavour is intense enough, strain through a coffee filter. Weigh the fermented cherry juice, then measure out 1.5% of that weight in sugar, 1% in citric acid, 0.5% in malic acid and 0.5% almond extract per 200 ml/6¾ fl oz. Stir in until dissolved. Bottle and store the cordial in the refrigerator for up to 3 weeks.

White Soy &
Watermelon Spritz

Watermelon works incredibly well with savoury flavours, and here it is paired with the earthy umami notes of white soy sauce to give a complex and moreish drink. White soy sauce is slightly milder than regular soy sauce, and is prized in Japan for its delicate flavour and pale colour. It's available in Japanese stores or online.

2.5 ml/½ teaspoon white soy sauce

10 ml/2 teaspoons sugar syrup (1:1 sugar to water ratio)

25 ml/¾ fl oz. watermelon juice

25 ml/¾ fl oz. vodka

soda water, to top up

watermelon slice, to garnish

Pour the white soy sauce, sugar syrup, watermelon juice and vodka into a tall glass tumbler over ice. Stir to mix the ingredients, then top up with soda water. Garnish with a watermelon slice.

Pickled Melon Gibson

Traditionally served with a pickled pearl onion on the side, this version of a classic gibson cocktail swaps the garnish for pickled melon balls.

40 ml/1⅓ fl oz. Nikka Coffey gin
20 ml/⅔ fl oz. dry vermouth (ideally Dolin Blanc)
Pickled Melon Balls*, to garnish

Place a small coupe glass in the freezer. Stir together the gin and vermouth over ice in a mixing glass for up to 1 minute. Strain into the frosted glass and garnish with the pickled melon balls on a cocktail stick/toothpick.

***Pickled Melon Balls:** 250 ml/1 cup plus 1 tablespoon rice wine vinegar, 50 ml/⅔ fl oz. mirin, 2 tablespoons caster/granulated sugar, 5 thin slices red chilli/chile, 1 teaspoon pink peppercorns, 10 g/2 teaspoons sea salt, ¼ honeydew melon, seeds removed, cut into balls using a melon baller Stir together all the ingredients (apart from the melon) in a mason/kilner jar to dissolve the sugar and salt. Add the melon balls, then seal the jar and leave at room temperature for 24 hours before refrigerating and leaving for a minimum of 1 week to pickle. The leftover pickled melon balls will keep in the brine for up to 3 weeks refrigerated.